From Rejection to Royalty

The Journey of
Dr. Nicole D. Reid

Divine Works Publishing, LLC
Royal Palm Beach, Fl

© 2025 DR. NICOLE D. REID

All Rights Reserved. No part of this publication may be reproduced, stored in a retrieval system, or transmitted in any form or by any means, electronic, mechanical, photocopying, recording or otherwise without the prior permission of the publisher or in accordance with the provisions of the Copyright, Designs, and Patents Act 1988 or under the terms of any license permitting limited copying issued by the Copyright Licensing Agency.

The views expressed in this work are solely those of the author and do not necessarily reflect the views of the publisher. The publisher hereby disclaims any responsibility for them.

ISBN: 978-1-949105-91-9 (paperback)
ISBN: 978-1-949105-92-6 (hardback)
ISBN: 978-1-949105-33-9 (eBook)
ISBN: 978-1-949105-90-2 (Audiobook)

First Edition Published: 09/01/2025
Printed: Royal Palm Beach, Florida, United States

Sources Cited: Scriptures by King James Version (KJV) unless otherwise noted.

Divine Works Publishing books are available at special discounts when purchased in quantity for premiums and promotions and for educational and fundraising use. For details, feel free contact us via email: books@divineworkspublishing.com or call the number listed below.

Published by:
Divine Works Publishing
Royal Palm Beach, Florida USA
www.DivineWorksPublishing.com
561-990-BOOK (2665)

The nations will see your vindication,
and all kings your glory;
you will be called by a new name
that the mouth of the Lord will bestow.
You will be a crown of splendor in the Lord's hand,
a royal diadem in the hand of your God.
No longer will they call you Deserted,
or name your land Desolate.
But you will be called Hephzibah,
and your land Beulah;
for the Lord will take delight in you,
and your land will be married.

Isaiah 62:2-4

Dedication

In loving dedication to
Mama Phyllis Anderson Lyon,
who raised me with love and sacrifice
from the moment I entered this world.

Picture of Mama   *My Son and I*

*The second image captures a defining moment in my early life—
me holding my first child, filled with love, hope, and uncertainty.*

Acknowledgments

I give all glory and honor to my Lord and Savior Jesus Christ, the Author and Finisher of my faith. Without Him, this story would not exist. His grace sustained me through the valleys and elevated me on mountaintops.

To Mama Phyllis Anderson Lyon—you were more than a caregiver; you were my first intercessor, my nurturer, and the foundation of my strength. I am eternally grateful for the love and discipline you instilled in me.

To my beloved children: Antwain, Shonari, and Amber and grandchildren David, Naomi and Ayanna—thank you for being my motivation when life felt too heavy. Your love pushed me to keep going.

To my loving husband, Dr. Barrington Reid, thank you for standing by me with patience, strength, and encouragement.

To Chief Apostle Dr. Kenneth L. Smith and Dr. Priscilla Smith—your mentorship, affirmation, and belief in my calling changed the trajectory of my life. Pastor Patricia Orange who was always there supporting, embracing and praying for me through my trials.

To my spiritual children, sons and daughters across the globe, the members, partners, the intercessors of Divine Connection Int'l Deliverance Ministry, the Fire Prayer Zoom family, and the Dr. Nicole Reid Foundation —

thank you for walking this journey with me. You are the fruit of this revelation.

Lastly, to every person who ever rejected me, misunderstood me, or walked away—thank you. You were part of the process God used to shape me. What was meant for evil, God turned for good. Shalom!!

Table of Contents

Dedication   iii

Acknowledgments   v

Foreword   ix

1 | Foundations of Grace   *1*

2 | Church, Chains, and Chastening   *5*

3 | Cracks in the Clay Pot   *11*

4 | Leaving Without My Heart   *15*

5 | The Comeback and the Call   *19*

6 | Closure, Discovery, & the Power of Forgiveness   *23*

7 | Revelation Realized   *27*

Conclusion: Keep the Faith   *31*

Prayer for Deliverance (Spirit of Rejection)   35

Apostolic Blessing for the Reader   45

About the Author   47

Foreword

by Dr. Barrington A. Reid

There are stories that entertain, and then there are stories that transform. This is one of those stories.

From Rejection to Royalty is not just a book — it is a testimony of triumph, a journey through darkness that leads to divine light. Apostle Dr. Nicole Reid's life is a living, breathing example of what God can do with someone the world has written off. With transparency, courage, and deep spiritual insight, she shares how pain became purpose, how isolation became intercession, and how rejection was only the beginning of her revelation.

You are not reading these pages by accident.

You were drawn to them by divine assignment.

Prepare to laugh, cry, reflect, and worship — and above all, prepare to see your own story through the lens of God's redemption.

Let this book speak to the child who was left behind, the woman who was overlooked, the leader who was broken, and the soul who is still waiting on a promise.

Apostle Dr. Nicole's life proves **God always keeps His promises.**

1
Foundations of Grace

I am Apostle Dr. Nicole Reid. My story began in the vibrant city of Montego Bay, Jamaica, where I was born — but my earliest roots took hold in a quiet, rural village called St. Simon, nestled in the heart of Hanover.

While many children are raised by their biological parents, my journey was different from the very beginning. When I was just one week old, I was placed in the loving care of my mother's family maid— a woman who despite her mental battles with Bi-polar Disorder displayed strength, resilience, and a nurturing spirit that helped shape the foundation of who I would become.

Her mood swings were difficult to navigate. There were times when she allowed me to attend church rehearsals in the evening, only for me to return home and find myself locked out. She would shout from inside, telling me to go sleep outside with the dogs. Then I would hear her stumbling through the darkness, torch light in hand, crying out, "Dawn, where are you?"

Sometimes, out of spite, I wouldn't answer. I'd hide among the flowers, listening to her weep and pray. Guilt would rise in me almost instantly. When I finally revealed myself, the relief on her face quickly turned into rage. She would beat me mercilessly. Once the blows began, the dogs would join in, attacking me too. Afterward, she bathed me in warm water, trying to reduce the swelling and conceal the bruises. At times the injuries were so severe, I ended up in the hospital from the dog bites.

The situation was made worse by an unspoken tension: my family, who led the church and nurtured my spiritual gifts, never helped her financially with things like church event outfits or other expenses. She bore that burden alone—and although she struggled, she still wanted me to look presentable among the other children.

The unpredictability of her disorder would emerge in other abusive ways; she would bite my ears at times, other times she would choke me or tie me to the bed rail.

Growing up in St. Simon, life was humble but full of silent blessings. I learnt early on that purpose doesn't wait for perfect conditions to begin revealing itself.

Nonetheless, even in the simplicity of my surroundings, God was planting seeds of calling, vision, and ministry deep within my spirit.

Rejection May

whisper that you're too small for purpose

But Royalty

*discloses how God plants greatness
in the hidden places.*

#FromRejectiontoRoyalty

2
Church, Chains, and Chastening

Growing up in a peaceful, rural Jamaican community, joy was often borrowed and brief. I found it in the simple things—music, dancing, and sunshine. The small hotspots in St. Simon were lit with the sounds of reggae, calypso, & diversified genres of american music. These rhythms became an escape from the silence of rejection and the weight of poverty. I would sing, dance, and lose myself in melodies that soothed my soul, only for a moment, but joy wasn't the only thing I found in those moments.

Teenage friends introduced me to marijuana. It started as curiosity. A moment of feeling included quickly became a trap. I was just a teenager, searching for peace and a place to belong. Church had become a place of judgment instead of refuge, so I walked away, bitter and bruised by rejection.

Yet even in rebellion, I couldn't escape the gift within. I had prophetic insight from an early age—I could feel people's hearts, know their intentions, and see things before they happened. My dreams were intense and often came to pass. It scared me. It separated me. I felt different, marked, and misunderstood.

Then one day, Mama confronted me. She found out I had been smoking, not only smoking but I began to plant marijuana on the property in nearby bushes. She was devastated. My adopted brother, who was a Rastafarian, came home and destroyed my small marijuana crop. I felt angry because I thought he would have supported me, knowing that it was a part of their religion, but he didn't. We fought by throwing stones at each other that day. I couldn't see that I was heading down the wrong path. He was only trying to protect me. Thank God for him. God used a rasta man to destroy my ganja crop, haha! I planted marijuana because I wanted to make money by selling it so that I could help myself, but God said not so. One day, I sat on the hillside of a playfield overlooking the ocean, lost in my thoughts. Suddenly, I heard an audible voice, clear and commanding say, "Stop what you're doing! Stop smoking! This isn't you!"

Startled, I looked around. No one was there.

2 / Church, Chains, and Chastening

Tears filled my eyes as I whispered, "God, if that's You, please take the craving from my taste buds." Within days, I had no appetite for marijuana. Even the smell made me nauseous. When I returned to the group, they mocked me. They gave me one week to return to the smoking gang. I never did.

God had delivered me, and I promised Him I wouldn't go back, but the attacks didn't end.

A relationship I had entered during my teenage years became violent and abusive. He believed I was vulnerable because he thought I had no father, no one to defend me. I tried to leave many times, but he kept pulling me back—sometimes with manipulation, other times with fists, kicks in a disgraceful manner, but I fought back forcefully with my battle armaments; sticks, stones and knives— cause I detested rubbish. Mama always told me not to take beatings from anyone. She gave me strategies on how to handle bullies, especially men who were physically abusive to women. Mama was physically strong and she knew how to defend herself. She taught me well.

Then came a breaking point.

It was time for CXC exams, the final tests that would determine our futures. The goats—my only financial resource—were gone. Neighbors had killed them because they were grazing in their crops. Mama had no more to give, and I had no more strength to stay.

I left my parish to find work and escape the abuse. Shortly after, I discovered I was pregnant—a consequence of a compromised situation I tried to avoid—I jumped out of a frying pan straight into the fire. My whole world was falling down.

The year was 1986. Our class had no graduation. We were punished as a group and were only allowed a valedictory service. I stood there in my school uniform, two months pregnant, with a brave face and a crushed heart.

No one knew my secret. Not even Mama. I didn't lose hope.

Mama stood by me when I shared the news of my pregnancy. On February 19, 1987, she stood by my hospital bed as I gave birth to my first son. I was now a teenage mother, but I was also a fighter, and God had more in store.

Rejection May

try to chain you to your past

But Royalty

unveils that despite the process God delivers his children.

#FromRejectiontoRoyalty

3

Cracks in the Claypot

After giving birth, I entered the working world in a tourist resort area as a tour coordinator. It was exciting, a glimpse of something beyond the hills of Hanover. I felt useful and confident—but beneath the surface, I was struggling.

I missed school. I missed my purpose. I missed dreaming. I wanted more, not just for me, but for my son.

Then came an unexpected shift—my biological grandmother, the one I hadn't known growing up, reached out to her friend in the community with a letter. She asked her to contact me and to forward her U.S.A. address and phone number to me. I was excited God didn't forget about me. I spoke to her briefly on the phone and she gave me my mother's phone number. They filed for my immigration documents to migrate permanently to the United States. Two and a half years later, the documents were approved, she came for me. I had a difficult decision to make.

They told me I couldn't take my baby.

They said I wouldn't afford daycare.

They told me to come and "start over."

But how do you start over without your heart?

I left my son with Mama and his father, heartbroken but determined. I boarded a plane to California with pain in my chest and purpose in my hands. I promised myself this sacrifice would one day bring him back to me, but what followed was a season of emotional drought.

My son's immigration file was archived for five and a half years.

I was told to forget him—to forget Mama.

But I couldn't. I wouldn't.

My biological mother, sisters, and I relocated to Florida after an earthquake shook California in early 1990. We moved together, but the tension grew. On March 20th, 1990, after refusing to cut off communication with Mama and my son, I came home from work one night in the rain to my place of abode and I was evicted into the rain.

I had nowhere to go.

God always has a ram in the bush.

A Jamaican young woman I had befriended on the job had given me her number. I called her. Without hesitation, she gave me shelter. It was the hand of God moving through His people. Still, Mama was worried—I had no way to update her.

One night, I was invited to a nightclub with my new friends to distract myself. There, I saw someone who would change everything—a friend of my cousin, who led me back to the extended family members that I once met when I came to live in Florida. I had no way of locating them because my diary was destroyed and I wasn't familiar with the area. I had no way of finding them but God directed my path even to the night club. They welcomed me. I was no longer alone.

By December 1990, I returned to Jamaica for the first time after my migration to the U.S.A in 1989.

I saw Mama and my son.

When I reached out to hug him, he pulled away.

He didn't know who I was. I heard him say to his little cousin "your mother is here" not knowing I was his mother.

It broke me but I had a plan—and I had God.

Rejection May

scatter what you love

But Royalty

restores what the enemy thought was lost forever..

#FromRejectiontoRoyalty

4
Leaving Without My Heart

When I returned to Florida from my first visit to my son, I set goals and earnestly pursued them.

I began working at a bank. Accounting was one of my majors in high school and that helped me. I had always been good with numbers. I was hungry for stability—not just for myself, but to one day bring my son home.

I wept in silence. My son was my joy, my purpose—my miracle, but I had to think of his future, and of what I could become. Mama and his father agreed to take care of him, and with my heart breaking it was one of the hardest decisions I ever had to make.

I entered a world that was fast, foreign, and often cold. The culture shock hit hard. I was trying to find my footing in a new land, all while grieving the separation from my child and the constant worry for mama. I would sit up nights wondering if they were okay, if my son missed me, and if mama had enough to feed him.

He went to live with his father but I received phone calls that were disturbing. I sent him back to the country to be with mama. I told mama not to send him back to his father but they reported mama to the police for kidnapping. I cried. I returned to Jamaica and filed a complaint at the family court. I lost. The court ruled in favor of his father. He was next of kin, I was living in the USA and mama was too old to handle him. I wept bitterly. He was traumatized because he loved mama. When I returned to the USA after the hearing, mama said the court sent police officers along with his father to retrieve my son.

My son ran away in the bushes. He was sobbing and bewildered. They caught him and he returned to the other parish where he was once living with his father. I sent clothes once per year in barrels but he didn't receive most of them. He had to share.

He was now rebelling. He started fires trying to burn his father's and his grandmother's house down. When asked why, he said he wanted his mom. They nick-named him "Fireman."

I cried, spoke to him sometimes on the phone but he seemed lost and in despair. He wanted to be with me and

4 / Leaving Without My Heart

I wanted to be with him. It wasn't possible. The immigration issues delayed his paperwork—five and a half years of waiting, hoping, and praying. I contacted congress for assistance but they couldn't help.

I was told to forget about him and mama, to focus on my new life in America but I could not and would not.

No degree, job, or success could fill the void of being separated from my child and the woman who raised me when no one else would.

Rejection May
seperate you from what you love

But Royalty

assures that God already paved the path for restoration.

#FromRejectiontoRoyalty

5

The Comeback and the Call

I was more determined than ever to change the course of my life—for my son, for mama, and for myself. I was naturally gifted in my strong foundation from high school. I excelled quickly. Numbers came easy to me, but it wasn't just about skill—it was purpose. I knew I had to stabilize my life to bring my son home.

I prayed often:

"Lord, if You help me get my own place, I promise I'll go back for my son."

In 1992, God answered. I got married and purchased a home that could accommodate my child.

On November 16, 1994 the miracle came full circle—my son arrived in the United States. After years of waiting, hoping, and believing, we were finally together. It was one of the happiest moments of my life.

But God wasn't finished with me yet.

That same year, I rededicated my life to Christ. On March 7, 1994, I surrendered fully, finally acknowledging the prophetic call I had felt since childhood. I said yes to God—not just in words, but with my life.

Soon after, I received a scholarship to attend Ft. Lauderdale Open Bible Institute. I studied with passion and purpose, graduating valedictorian with numerous distinctions in theology. I knew then that ministry wasn't just an option—it was destiny. Still, I found myself torn between two practical careers: nursing or cosmetology. I tested both, becoming a Registered Nurse, but it didn't sit right in my spirit. So I followed my creative gift and became a licensed cosmetologist in 1999.

Cosmetology gave me the flexibility to raise my children, attend church, minister, and study the Word. I was now a mother of three—two boys and a daughter—and the Lord was shaping me into the vessel He always intended.

I went deeper. I committed seven years to apostolic and prophetic leadership training. I went on to earn a PhD in Christian Counseling at Smith Christian University in Fort Lauderdale, Florida. I began to travel extensively—across the Caribbean, the United States, the United

5 / The Comeback and the Call

Kingdom, and Africa—preaching, prophesying, feeding the hungry, and caring for widows and orphans.

In 2018, during a mission trip to Cameroon, I witnessed one of the greatest miracles of my life. I prayed for a woman whose baby had died shortly after birth. The baby came back to life—after ten minutes. That family named the child after me—they gave her my first and last name—in honor of what God did. To this day, I continue to support them whenever I can.

God birthed in me several ministries:

- Divine Connection Int'l Deliverance Ministry
- Fire Prayer Zoom Platform
- New Dawn Revelation Counseling Inc.
- OBIM Consulting Solutions, LLC.
- Boutique La Africa
- Dr. Nicole Reid Foundation

I am not only a confirmed prophetess but also an affirmed apostle— however I hold this truth close:

"God isn't impressed by your titles, but by your character, your obedience, and your faith."

Rejection May
delay your dreams

But Royalty

reassures that God fulfills them in His perfect time and calls you higher than you imagined.

#FromRejectiontoRoyalty

6
Closure, Discovery, & the Power of Forgiveness

Before her passing, mama—Phyllis Anderson Lyon—received the reward of her labor. She was granted a 10-year visa and visited the United States twice, meeting her grandchildren, walking through the house I had bought, and experiencing the joy of the life she had sown into.

On July 27, 2003, at the age of 89, mama went home to be with the Lord. I honored her life with a beautiful homegoing celebration, fit for the queen that she was. Her absence left a void, but I was filled with gratitude. She had witnessed the fruit of her love, sacrifice, and prayers.

Just when I thought the past was sealed, God opened a new chapter.

For years, I didn't know who my father was, but through a modern miracle called DNA testing database—specifically 23andMe—I discovered the truth. The results connected me with a half-brother, who led me to four more siblings. My heart beat faster as I learnt more. I am the first child of six. We had a unification celebration.

My biological father had been a headmaster and teacher for over 20 years. His name was known in educational circles. He had passed away in 2001, never knowing I existed—his firstborn child. I was overcome with emotion when I visited his grave at Maple Grove Cemetery in New York. Though we never met in life, I finally had closure.

The discoveries didn't stop there. I found aunties, an uncle, and cousins—many of whom I had grown up around in Jamaica without knowing they were blood relatives. My father's siblings are living in the UK, his mom and dad passed away and were buried there. My eldest aunt and her son came to visit me in the U.S. The mystery was gone. The rejection was broken. My identity was restored.

But none of these stories would be complete without acknowledging the greatest healing of all—forgiveness.

Despite the pain of abandonment and misunderstanding, I found healing through forgiveness. I chose to forgive my biological mother. She, too, had been traumatized. Her decisions may have hurt me, but I realized they were made out of fear, confusion, and brokenness.

I forgave her completely, and I can truly say, I love her.

That forgiveness freed me.

It unchained me from the cycle of rejection, and it allowed me to walk into the fullness of revelation—not just of who I am, but of who God created me to be.

Rejection May
leave questions unanswered

But Royalty
reveals the truth that heals and the grace that forgives.

#FromRejectiontoRoyalty

7
Revelation Realized

My life is a mosaic of the broken and the beautiful—each piece hand-placed by the Master's design.

What began in rejection, poverty, abandonment, abuse and obscurity was always meant to lead me into revelation, purpose, and global impact. From a one-week old baby left in the arms of a maid, to an international apostle and advocate for the broken, I am living proof that God never wastes pain.

I have preached the gospel across continents, seen a dead baby revived, watched widows fed, and laid hands on the forgotten and forsaken. I have founded ministries, educated leaders, raised children, and birthed purpose through obedience.

I am the fruit of Mama's prayers, the answer to her tears, and the evidence that God sees the lowly. Her love, even when wrapped in pain, became the soil where God planted a prophet.

I am a voice for the voiceless, a mother to nations, and a midwife to destinies.

Through the Divine Connection International Deliverance Ministry, the Fire Prayer Zoom platform, New Dawn Revelation Counseling Inc., and the Dr. Nicole Reid Foundation, I continue to serve with the same fire that lit me on a Jamaican hillside when God first spoke to me.

I don't boast in titles. I boast in grace. I boast in obedience. I boast in the faithfulness of a God who found me in the dark and called me His own.

Rejection May

try to silence your voice

But Royalty

declares you a voice to nations and a witness of God's faithfulness.

#FromRejectiontoRoyalty

Conlusion

Keep the Faith

To every person reading these words—whether you were abandoned, abused, misunderstood, or overlooked—know this:

You are not forgotten.

Your pain is not wasted.

Your story is still being written.

Forgiveness is not weakness—it is freedom.

Obedience is not sacrifice—it is alignment.

And rejection is not your ending—it's the hallway to revelation.

If God did it for me, He will do it for you.

Keep praying.

Keep believing.

Keep the faith.

Because He will never leave you nor forsake you.

I am Apostle Dr. Nicole D. Reid,
And this is my story—
From Rejection to Royalty.

From Rejection

To Royalty

Prayer for Deliverance from the Spirit of Rejection

Father God,

In the mighty and matchless name of Jesus Christ, I come boldly before Your throne of grace on behalf of every heart crying out for freedom. Lord, You are the Alpha and the Omega — You saw our beginning, and You have already declared our end. Nothing is hidden from Your sight.

Right now, in the authority of Jesus Christ, I address every deep-seated root of rejection — rejection from the family lineage, from the womb, from birth, from childhood, and from the traumas of adulthood. I uproot every seed, every root, every branch, and every fruit of rejection that has grown in the soul.

Lord, I expose and renounce:
- Rejection from parents, (spoken or unspoken).
- Abandonment and emotional neglect.
- Words that cursed identity.
- The silent treatments, exclusions, favoritisms, and any and all comparisons.
- Abuse — physical, verbal, emotional, sexual.
- Every lie that said, "You are not enough," "You are unwanted," or "You are a mistake."
- Every generational cycle where rejection passed down like an inheritance.
- By the blood of Jesus, I sever the cord between my soul and every demonic attachment that entered through rejection. I declare that the access points are closed, and the legal rights of the enemy are canceled by the finished work of the cross.

Spirit of rejection, I command you to leave now — every residue, every manifestation:

- Low self-worth
- Constant need for approval
- Fear of abandonment
- Overcompensating for love
- People-pleasing
- Self-sabotage
- Isolation and withdrawal

- Bitterness and resentment
- Unforgiveness
- Cycles of broken relationships
- Difficulty trusting others or receiving love

You will not return. Go now, in the name of Jesus!

Lord, I ask You to cleanse the soul now— the mind, will, and emotions with the purifying fire of the Holy Spirit. Wash away the residue of every negative word, every false identity, every image that is not aligned with Heaven's blueprint. Dislodge every automatic negative thought that has set itself against the knowledge of Christ. Let the light of *Your Truth* flood every hidden place.

I declare a new identity to take root:

+ Beloved child of God.
+ Fearfully and wonderfully made.
+ Chosen before the foundation of the world.
+ A royal priesthood, a holy nation.
+ An heir of God and joint-heir with Christ.
+ Seated in heavenly places.

Holy Spirit, fill every void now — every gap left by rejection — with Your power, Your love, Your comfort, and Your truth. Let the oil of gladness replace mourning, and the garment of praise replace the spirit of heaviness.

Lord, reveal to them their highest purpose — why they were intentionally created, and the nations, lives, and generations tied to their obedience. I declare that they will rise as voices in the earth, carrying the message of reconciliation, healing, and their true identity in Christ.

I seal this prayer in the blood of Jesus and declare that whom the Son sets free is free indeed. The spirit of rejection will no longer define, confine, or bind them. They are loved. They are accepted in the Beloved. They are chosen for such a time as this.

In Jesus' name, Amen.

30 Days
of Deliverance Declarations

(To be spoken aloud daily, preferably morning and night)

For the next **30 Days** seal your deliverance with the daily declarations on the following pages. These are provided to reinforce your renewed understanding and to transform your old patterns of thinking into the higher truths found within the word of God.

Week 1 – Identity in Christ
(Days 1–7)

I am accepted in the Beloved;
rejection has no claim on me.
(Ephesians 1:6)

I am fearfully and wonderfully made;
God makes no mistakes.
(Psalm 139:14)

Before I was formed in the womb,
God knew me and set me apart.
(Jeremiah 1:5)

I am chosen, royal, and holy in God's eyes.
(1 Peter 2:9)

God calls me by my true name,
not by the labels of people.
(Isaiah 43:1)

My worth is determined by the blood of Jesus,
not human opinion.
(1 Corinthians 6:20)

I am a new creation;
old things have passed away.
(2 Corinthians 5:17)

Week 2 – Breaking Agreement with Lies (Days 8–14)

*I renounce every lie that says I am
or ever was unworthy or unwanted.*
(John 8:44)

*I break every generational curse of rejection
in my bloodline.*
(Galatians 3:13)

*I will not live in fear of abandonment;
God will never leave me.*
(Deuteronomy 31:6)

*I silence every voice that contradicts
God's truth over my life.*
(2 Corinthians 10:5)

*My value is not measured by people's acceptance,
but by God's love.*
(Romans 8:38–39)

*I refuse to perform for love;
I am already loved unconditionally.*
(1 John 3:1)

*I uproot every seed of self-sabotage
and plant seeds of destiny instead.*
(Matthew 15:13)

Week 3 – Healing the Soul
(Days 15–21)

My mind is renewed by the Word of God daily.
(Romans 12:2)

My emotions are anchored in the peace of Christ.
(Colossians 3:15)

My will aligns with God's perfect plan for my life.
(Psalm 143:10)

*I forgive those who rejected me;
I release them into God's hands.* (Ephesians 4:32)

I bless my past, knowing God will use it for my good.
(Romans 8:28)

*I release every heavy burden and receive the joy of
the Lord.* (Matthew 11:28–30)

I choose love over bitterness and purpose over pain.
(Hebrews 12:15)

My life is a testimony of God's faithfulness.
(Psalm 40:3)

Week 4 – Walking in Purpose (Days 22–30)

I am a voice to the nations and a light in the darkness.
(Matthew 5:14)

I carry the message of healing and reconciliation.
(2 Corinthians 5:18)

I am equipped and anointed for every assignment God gives me. (Isaiah 61:1)

I will not shrink back; I will walk boldly in my calling.
(Hebrews 10:39)

I will fulfill my purpose and complete my God-given mission. (Acts 20:24)

I am a restorer of broken walls and a rebuilder of ancient ruins. (Isaiah 58:12)

Nations will be blessed because I said yes to God.
(Genesis 12:2–3)

I am free, whole, loved, and unshakable in Christ.
(John 8:36)

An Apostolic Blessing for the reader
By Apostle Dr. Nicole Reid

*Father, I pray for the one reading this book —
that they will be encouraged and know that You, Lord,
are omnipotent, omniscient, and omnipresent.*

*I pray that as they read, You will begin to change
their story in the name of Jesus.*

*I decree and declare that You will intervene in their
situation and bring forth miracles and
great testimonies, in Jesus' name.*

*I declare them blessed, highly favored,
and covered under the blood of Jesus.*

*I decree and declare their lives will never again be
the same but will exude your extraordinary glory.*

Let Your holy fire envelope their entire being.

*In the mighty name of Jesus Christ,
Amen.*

About the Author

Apostle Dr. Nicole Reid is a globally affirmed apostle, prophetess, counselor, teacher, founder and overseer of multiple ministries that serve the Body of Christ with love, fire, and purpose. She holds a PhD in Christian Counseling and is the founder of:

- Divine Connection Int'l Deliverance Ministry
- Fire Prayer Zoom Platform
- New Dawn Revelation Counseling Inc.
- The Dr. Nicole Reid Foundation
- Boutique La Africa
- OBIM Consulting Solutions LLC

She has traveled across the Caribbean, Africa, the United Kingdom, and the United States extensively, preaching, prophesying, and carrying healing and deliverance to those in need. Her heart is especially drawn to widows, orphans, and the rejected, as she ministers with deep compassion and power.

She is a spiritual mother to many, a mentor to rising leaders, and a living testimony of Isaiah 61:1–3.

The Spirit of the Lord GOD is upon me; because the Lord hath anointed me to preach good tidings unto the meek; he hath sent me to bind up the brokenhearted, to proclaim liberty to the captives, and the opening of the prison to them that are bound;

To proclaim the acceptable year of the Lord, and the day of vengeance of our God; to comfort all that mourn;

To appoint unto them that mourn in Zion, to give unto them beauty for ashes, the oil of joy for mourning, the garment of praise for the spirit of heaviness; that they might be called trees of righteousness, the planting of the Lord, that he might be glorified.

–Isaiah 61:1–3 (KJV)

About
Divine Connection International Deliverance Ministry

Divine Connection International Deliverance Ministry was birthed out of my own journey with God and the burning desire He placed in my heart to see people set free. It was founded on August 7, 2013 Fort Lauderdale Florida. For many years, I carried the weight of rejection, pain, and spiritual battles, but it was in those seasons that God showed me His power to heal and deliver. Out of those experiences came the calling to create a ministry that would not only preach the Word but also break the yokes that keep God's people in bondage.

When I answered the call, I did not fully know the magnitude of what God was doing, but I knew He wanted me to build a ministry where people could encounter His power and presence. Divine Connection became that place—a space where prayer, intercession, and deliverance are not just practiced but lived out daily. From small gatherings to international platforms, I have watched the Lord use this ministry to touch lives across nations, bringing healing to the brokenhearted and liberty to those who were oppressed.

This ministry is not just an organization; it is my life's assignment. Every testimony of a soul saved, a family restored, or a life transformed is evidence of God's faithfulness. Through Divine Connection International

Deliverance Ministry, God has proven that what the enemy meant for harm, He can turn into a global assignment for His glory. What started as a vision in prayer has now become a movement impacting lives far beyond what I ever imagined.

About
Fire Prayer Zoom Call

During the early stages of Divine Connection International Deliverance Ministry, the Lord gave me another assignment that would extend beyond physical walls – **The Fire Prayer Zoom Platform.** "The place where miracles happen." What started as a simple act of obedience quickly became a global altar of prayer. At first, I saw it only as a way to keep believers connected, but God revealed that it would be a lifeline for people across nations who were hungry for prayer, healing, and deliverance.

Through the Fire Prayer Platform, I have witnessed firsthand the power of unity in prayer. Week after week, men and women from different countries log in—not bound by distance or culture, but united by a deep desire to seek the face of God. On this platform, burdens are lifted, chains are broken, and miracles are released.

There have been testimonies of healing, breakthrough in impossible situations, and even restoration in families who had given up hope.

For me, the Fire Prayer Zoom Platform is more than just a virtual meeting; it is a move of God for this generation. It proves that prayer has no boundaries, and the fire of the Holy Spirit can reach living rooms, hospital rooms, and workplaces across the world. I am humbled every time I see God use this platform to ignite revival in the hearts of His people. What the enemy thought would be a tool of isolation in a digital age, God has transformed into a channel of fire, connection, and deliverance.

About
New Dawn Revelation Counseling Ministry

Out of my own experiences of pain, rejection, and restoration, the Lord birthed another assignment in me—**New Dawn Revelation Counseling Ministry**. This counseling ministry was created to bring healing to the mind, soul, and spirit. Many times, people carry wounds that are not visible to the eye, but they affect every part of their lives. God placed it on my heart to walk alongside those who are broken, guiding them with biblical counseling, wisdom, and compassion.

New Dawn Revelation Counseling Ministry is more than a program; it is a safe place where people can confront the hurts of the past and step into the hope of a new beginning. Through one-on-one sessions, group support, and faith-based guidance, I have witnessed God restore confidence to the discouraged, peace to the anxious, and clarity to the confused. The name New Dawn Revelation is intentional—Dawn is my middle name, it represents a fresh start, a new morning filled with light after a long night of darkness.

This ministry is deeply personal to me, because I know what it means to feel broken yet called by God. Every counseling session reminds me that healing is possible, deliverance is available, and transformation is real. God uses New Dawn Revelation to bring wholeness, not only to individuals, but also to families and communities. It is my joy to watch lives take on new meaning when the truth of God's Word brings revelation, and hope shines again like the dawn of a new day.

About
Dr. Nicole Reid Foundation

As the Lord continued to expand my assignments, He placed another vision on my heart—one that would go beyond the pulpit and counseling room and reach into the everyday needs of people. This is how the **Dr. Nicole Reid Foundation** was born. The foundation is built on compassion, service, and empowerment, providing support to those who are vulnerable, overlooked, and in need of a helping hand. This foundation has placed a permanent smile on children across the globe, especially during back to school.

From feeding programs and clothing drives to supporting education and community development, the foundation stands as an extension of my ministry, demonstrating the love of Christ through action. I believe the Gospel must be both preached and lived, and the foundation is one way God allows me to put faith into practice. Every act of kindness, whether big or small, is a seed sown into someone's future.

The Dr. Nicole Reid Foundation is not about me—it is about leaving a legacy of hope, especially for the next generation. My desire is that people will not only receive immediate help but also be equipped with tools to build better lives. Whether it is through mentorship, scholarships, or outreach projects, the foundation's mission is to restore dignity and inspire transformation. For me, this assignment is proof that ministry is not confined to church walls; it is about touching lives wherever there is need

About
Boutique La Africa

Alongside ministry and counseling, God also birthed in me a passion for entrepreneurship and creativity. This passion gave life to **Boutique La Africa**, a fashion boutique that celebrates culture, beauty, and confidence. For me, Boutique La Africa is not just about clothing—it is about identity. It reflects the strength and elegance of African heritage while also embracing modern style, allowing women to feel empowered, unique, and unapologetically themselves.

This is more than a business; it turned into a platform of expression. I wanted every client who connected with my authentic African attire —feel, seen, valued, and inspired. Through Boutique La Africa, I have been able to merge creativity with purpose, using fashion as a way to uplift others. Many who shopped with us did not just leave with garments—they left with renewed confidence, carrying a piece of cultural pride with them.

This venture reminded me that God places gifts in us that can manifest in many forms. Ministry can be preaching and counseling, but it can also be creating opportunities, jobs, and inspiration through business. Boutique La Africa has been one of those assignments where I saw that serving God is not limited to the church—it extends into how we use our talents to impact the world. Many people are blessed by the quality and beauty of the variety of African fashion during black history month.

About
OBIM'S Consulting Solutions, LLC

In addition to ministry and counseling, the Lord opened doors for me in the area of business and professional development through **OBIM'S Consulting Solutions LLC.** This company was established to provide guidance, strategies, and solutions for individuals and organizations seeking growth, stability, and excellence. I realized that many people had potential but lacked the proper tools, structure, and vision to reach their goals. OBIM'S became the platform where I could use my experience, skills, and God-given wisdom to help them succeed.

Through OBIM'S Consulting Solutions, I have worked with clients in areas such as business development, organizational strategy, and personal growth. For me, consulting is more than offering advice—it is about empowering people with practical steps to achieve lasting success. Each session is an opportunity to equip leaders, inspire innovation, and build systems that not only meet immediate needs but also prepare for future growth.

What makes OBIM'S unique is that it carries the same heart of ministry—service, excellence, and transformation. Whether it is helping a small business owner structure their vision, guiding a nonprofit into greater impact, or coaching individuals to embrace their God-given potential.

OBIM'S Consulting Solutions is a testament that God's purpose for my life goes beyond the pulpit. It proves that with faith and diligence, we can make a mark both spiritually and professionally, leaving behind a legacy of impact in multiple arenas.

Contact

Ministry Contact Information

Divine Connection International Deliverance Ministry Inc.

Booking Requests:

To requests Apostle Dr. Nicole D. Reid for speaking engagements:

Phone: 954-600-3186

Email: NDELR1125@gmail.com

Connect with Dr. Nicole D. Reid
on Social Media

Facebook
@Divine Connection Int'l Deliverance Ministry

Instagram
@Divine Connection Int'l Deliverance

YouTube
@nicolemitchell9212

TikTok
@reidy112

YOU WRITE,
WE PUBLISH,
TOGETHER WE CREATE

DIVINE WORKS PUBLISHING, LLC.

We publish to inspire, inform, and transform—because your story was made to move hearts and shift minds.

At Divine Works Publishing, we publish purpose-driven writers and help bring their message to life.

www.DivineWorksPublishing.com

561-990-BOOK (2665)

info@DivineWorksPublishing.com

www.ingramcontent.com/pod-product-compliance
Lightning Source LLC
Chambersburg PA
CBHW070241090526
44586CB00035B/1433